Maria

MYSTERY AND TEARS OF PENANCE

by Maria Gniotek

DORRANCE PUBLISHING CO
EST. 1920
PITTSBURGH, PENNSYLVANIA 15238

Dorrance Publishing Co
585 Alpha Drive
Pittsburgh, PA 15238
Visit our website at *www.dorrancebookstore.com*

ISBN: 978-8-8902-7290-4
eISBN: 978-8-8902-7788-6

Maria

Mystery and Tears of Penance

THE FOLLOWING IS BASED ON TRUE
EVENTS THAT HAPPENED
THROUGHOUT MY LIFE.

Chapter 1

My name is Maria. I was born in a small village in Poland called Kosmow in 1950. I had four brothers, one sister, a mother, and stepfather.

In 1972, I moved to Canada. I was twenty-two years old. I came to live with my aunt up north. One year later, I moved to Toronto. That's where I met my first love, who was Italian. He had tempting eyes. When I met Tony, I was twenty-three years old. He could not believe that I was still pure. He taught me love, beautiful love. At that time, he was the love of my life. At least, I thought he was. He was very good to me, gentle and kind. He took me to many places. It was like I was living in a dream.

He was very jealous. On car rides, he liked to pull my hair gently as I looked out the window. Quite often, I would close my eyes for a moment when I was with him in the car. Then he would stop the car so I would open my eyes. It was scary for me. I was in a couple of car accidents with him. The first accident occurred about half a year into our relationship. We went through a yellow light and crashed into another car. We ended up in a ditch. The left half of my body was severely bruised. Nothing happened to Tony, but I healed fast. My life continued with him.

The second accident with him was a year and a half later. While coming back from his friends' place, I fell asleep in the car. Unfortunately, I didn't have my seatbelt on, as it was not required at the time. I don't know what speed he was going and I don't know if his eyes were open or not, but he hit another car. The severe pain woke me up when I hit the windshield. The glass shattered into small pieces, and the front of the car was like an accordion. I screamed that he wanted to kill me. Nothing happened to him. I knew he was scared. He pointed his finger at me for me to be quiet, but I screamed until the ambulance came. I didn't have any abrasions on my head. They said I might have had a small concussion. I don't know how I got home that night.

The next day, I went to work at Fabricland, where I worked as a salesperson. Unfortunately, I had to go home because I wasn't feeling good. The next day, an insurance representative visited me, but I told him I did not want any money because Tony was my boyfriend and I loved him. He repeated the idea about getting insurance money, and I said the same thing, and finally, he left. That evening, my boyfriend came over and he told me with a smile on his face, "You are a tough Polack, and it is hard to kill you." I was covered with tears as my emotions grew. He noticed and tried to calm me down, he apologized and kissed me.

My mom came from Poland for a visit. She asked him if he was planning to marry me, and he responded yes. He bought a condominium and a sports car. I wasn't sure how, but I always had a feeling that it was from the insurance money. I was left with the pain. After my mom left, he told me it would be better if I didn't marry him because one of us would end up falling off the balcony. I had no idea what was going through his mind. Was he planning to kill me? It was then that I knew that if I stayed with him, I would die.

Things were not the same after that. Everything began falling apart. We didn't see each other too often. It was hard, but after three years I decided to leave him because it caused more pain to stay with him. I loved him, but he didn't love me. He had black eyes, tempting and shiny. Sometimes, he called, but I didn't want to see him. He always called me Marysia.

In time, I met a man at a dance. He was much older than me and his name was Romeo. He was very intelligent and a true gentleman. I was ready to dedicate my life to him because he treated me like a lady. His friend told me he was planning a surprise for me. Suddenly, Tony came to me with the biggest bouquet of flowers I had ever seen. He begged me on his knees to forgive him. His tempting eyes blinded me.

I called Romeo and said, "Forgive me, but I'm going back to my ex-boyfriend."

He told me politely and sadly, "Remember this. You're never going to be with him, and you will never see me again."

I had his number somewhere, but I could never find it after that day. It was as if it had vanished.

I eventually left Tony. Every time I wanted to meet somebody, Tony would call and reappear in my life, and everything would fall apart. Who was he? Who was the man I had such a beautiful love with? We had all those accidents, but he was never hurt, only me. To him, I was nothing more than a sex toy. Maybe God knew who he was and helped me leave him. After many years, I could never erase Tony from my mind, especially the words he said to me: "You are a tough Polack, and it is hard to kill you." Did he really try to kill me? It hurts so much when I think about that.

I knelt in front of the picture of Jesus, and I swore that I would never get married. I always said to myself that I would never marry a man who was divorced or Polish. I decided to go to Poland to forget about Tony. That was in 1977. I flew from Toronto to Montreal, where I had a layover. While waiting for my plane, I met a young man who was observing me. As he came up to me, I caught only a glimpse of his face before he sat down on the bench next to me. I noticed he was dressed up nicely in a light blue suit. As he talked to me, his head was facing forward and down. I only saw his side profile. He told me his name was Mark and he was of Polish descent. I told him my name, and he said he was going to Warsaw for three weeks. He said he had studied to become a lawyer. I thought, *Great. I don't have an education. What can I offer you? My love?* I gave him my phone number at the end of our conversation. I don't remember him writing my phone number down, and I don't remember seeing him on the plane.

I was in Poland for five weeks. After I returned from Poland, I had a vision that God was sending me on a mission with Mark. To love him, guide him, and protect him. A vision of touching the tears on my face with both hands, and placing them on Mark's face, telling him, "These are tears of love I am sending you; I want you to heal." I gently blew these tears towards him. I also received a curse, the kiss of death. I could not understand why God gave me this vision. I never confided in anybody; I didn't have anybody to talk to.

Mark called; he told me he was going to be in Toronto and asked if I could see him. I said yes. I was ready to see him. His voice was like that of a true man when he said my name. It sounded beautiful and made me emotional. I felt like I was blessed. Then my ex-boyfriend called, he wanted to see me. He asked me why I didn't ask him for money.

"I never ask you for money. If you knew I had money, you would marry me," I replied and hung up the phone.

I was visited by a man I worked with before I went to Poland. His eyes were shiny and fake. I saw him a couple of times, but there was no connection. The next day, I thought again about how Mark had studied to be a lawyer while I had no education. I felt as if there was something holding me back from him. Then I thought that it was not I who had chosen him, but that God had chosen him for me. But who was I to speak the words of God? I was confused.

Two days later, Mark called and said he was in Toronto, and he asked if I could see him.

I quickly told him, "I cannot see you. I have a boyfriend."

A second passed, and he replied, "Hmmm."

During my conversation with Mark, I heard the voice of children whispering the address of the place where I lived at the time.

I said, "Sorry, Mark," and I hung up the phone.

It was so fast that I didn't even ask for his number or where he was.

After I hung up, I shook and said, "What have I done? Where am I going to find him? Toronto is so big."

I didn't go outside too often. Almost two weeks passed, and I decided to meet up with my friend. I asked if she knew any single men. I knew she rented rooms out.

Her husband said to me, "The guys here are ugly. They are not for you."

She only knew a divorced man named Mitch and arranged for us to meet.

As I was coming home that night around 9:30 pm, I suddenly felt that someone was walking behind me. I turned to see who it was. Although the streetlights were on, it was dark. I saw a person hiding, but I continued walking. I passed the lights on Queen Street, and shortly after, I was on the veranda of the house where I was renting the third floor.

That's how it started. I knew right away that it was him. I thought to myself, *Mark, it's you. I know it's you. I can feel you, and I can feel your pain. Please do not hurt me. I know you have a temper. If you hurt me, you will never see me again. I will tell you who I am. I am the one chosen by God for you. God chose me to go on a mission with you, to love you, guide you, and protect you. I have a great power of love; my love is a healing love."* Something was preventing me from seeing him. I don't know what it was. Was it a curse or an evil spirit? If it were an evil spirit, I would have to say, "Evil spirit, leave me alone and go back to where you came from," three times, and then I would throw the kiss of death at the spirit. I'd been told that his eyes were different and would change after our first love.

Suddenly, I heard a woman's voice gently say to me in English, "Maria, do it. You're going to have a beautiful life. You don't have anybody. Do it. Try it for at least a day. Maria, you are going to regret this for the rest of your life. Do it!" And then she repeated, "Maria, protect him," at least three times.

My answer was, "I don't care."

I stood there stubbornly. I thought that if this were Mark, he would say something.

Once again, the voice said, "Maria, protect him."

It then disappeared, and I was left confused. I opened the door quickly and went inside.

He raced into the hallway and closed the door. He hit me in the head twice with his fist.

I said, "What do you want, money? I don't have any""

Suddenly, he became more aggressive, and he beat me brutally with triple the strength. He didn't have mercy; he punched me in the head with his fist. I called God for help. He stopped and went outside. A passerby stopped him. Apparently, they had heard what was going on, and he asked if everything was okay.

My attacker said, "Yes."

I could read their lips. I didn't say anything,

I was one hundred percent sure that he was Mark. I thought, *What kind of lawyer are you going to be if you're hitting people?* I felt my head begin to swell. Due to my pain and anger, I threw a curse at him, the "kiss of death," so he wouldn't be able to die without my forgiveness. I blew it gently. He ran off. I went into my apartment, confused by the pain.

The next day, I was ready to forgive him and take back the curse. Nobody else would be able to remove the curse except for me with a kiss. That's how powerful it was.

I thought about him quite often. Why had he beaten me? Why hadn't he come to ask me why I didn't want to see him? I regretted what

I had done, and I asked myself many questions. Was I stubborn, or had an evil spirit gotten inside me? It was stuck in my head that I had to get married that year. It was like I was possessed. I even forgot about the promise I had made to God that I would never get married.

Chapter 2

Mitch wanted to see me, so I met with him. We went out the next day and he kissed me.

A week later I went out with him again and I told him, "Buy me a ring."

I was joking, but he went and bought a ring.

The lady I was renting my place from said, "Don't do it. You are blind."

But I was too embarrassed to leave him. I think Satan took over. I got married a month and a half later. It was not a marriage of love, but one of need. My husband told me that if I left him, he would kill me. I looked at him and wondered why he would say that. Life continued in a good way.

I gave birth to my son a year later. Not even two years later, I gave birth to my daughter. I had my tubes tied so I wouldn't have any more kids. I didn't want to make love to him; I got no satisfaction from it. I was weak, and I didn't have anybody here. I did everything by myself. The truth is that my husband was good to me. It's just that something inside me felt different.

When my son was about three years old and my daughter about a year, we were renting a townhouse and I was sitting in the kitchen.

Suddenly, I felt as if a silver bullet had flown through my head. I immediately felt extreme pain in the back of my head. Then something started crawling under my skin and down my back. I didn't know what it was. I was shocked, but I didn't ask any questions. I was scared, living in that house. I didn't like it, especially the basement. When I went to do the laundry, it was as if I had entered a different zone. It was extremely cold in there. I always felt there was some kind of paranormal activity. I didn't tell anyone about it.

Time passed, and in the beginning of January 2014, I felt very cold, to the point that sometimes I found myself wearing a winter coat in the house.

Sometime during the middle of January, I was watching TV, and suddenly I heard a voice say, "Maria, forgive me."

I was shocked. Mark was dying and he had come for my forgiveness.

I said, "Mark, you beat me severely."

He replied, "Yes, I know, I know. But please forgive me."

I told him, "You are forgiven," and the voice disappeared.

I had forgiven him a long time before, but I could not remove the curse, as I had to see him and kiss him because that's how powerful the curse was. I was shaking because at this moment, I didn't know who I was. I never believed this was going to happen. I lit a candle and began praying the rosary.

The next day, in church as I was praying for him, my eyes began to fill with tears as I made peace with him. It was as though I could feel that he was dead. I cried and repeated the words I was supposed to say to him. Day after day, I repeated the same words with the candle, feeling his pain and talking to him. I started to smoke two packs a day and began drinking. I was covered with tears and losing my mind. I didn't know what to do. The picture of his visit played in front of my eyes, him beating me and the curse. I felt that his lost soul was with me. He was giving me signs. One of them was a plastic button popping off the sofa and rolling on the floor. I knew he was with me, and I prayed constantly. I had a pain in my stomach every day. I could not find a place to be, and I thought I was going crazy.

After thirty days, his presence was gone. I prayed in front of the picture of the Holy Mother holding Jesus. I knelt before it, begging for forgiveness and help. I lay on the floor with my arms open, begging for forgiveness in front of the beautiful icon of the Holy Mother and asking for her to take me away from this world. Nothing made me happy; my heart was breaking.

I decided to help myself by buying a spiritual book to heal. My husband's granddaughter, from his first marriage, offered to take me to a special store and she did. As we approached, the sign said, "spiritual shop." We went inside and I got a little scared. I looked around and to me, it seemed more like a witchcraft store. I talked to a young man and another man who was older. I tried to tell them what happened to me and that I had thrown a curse.

The older man whispered to the young man, and then he said to me, "You are one of us, and you are not going to die that quickly."

I was afraid to touch the books of witchcraft but at the same time I was intrigued to know what they contained.

He took us downstairs to a room, and I told him, "I am Catholic, and I believe in God."

He showed me his cellphone and a picture of the Holy Mother hanging in his house. He was a warlock and specialized in black magic. I bought a special package that contained two pieces of paper, a feather pen, smoked blood, and two black candles.

I came home and didn't know what to do. I felt Mark's pain every day. My conscience was bothering me, and my eyes filled with tears. I didn't know what to do. I laid on the couch and covered my eyes, trying to think of how beautiful life would have been with Mark. I told my sister everything that has happened, and she asked me why I had done that. My answer was, "I don't know." What had happened to me?

A friend of mine understood because she'd had an experience with a ghost. Another friend told me Mark would have hit me all the time, that I should forget about him. She didn't understand; my mind was the same. I had a feeling that Mark had been killed.

Every evening, I sat with the candle, asking him, "Who killed you? Come and tell me. Move the flame. Give me some kind of sign."

Every night, I felt worse. I could not sleep at night and instead, I drank coffee. I could feel his pain every day, and I asked him to tell me who had killed him.

Near the end of March 2014, around five o'clock in the morning, I finished my prayers and went for a smoke. I put my head on the door and had tears in my eyes. I had a small vision of an angelic choir that reassured me that I had been chosen by God. Three men with long grey hair wearing beautiful white overcoats with dark embroidery and large instruments. They could see me. One of the instruments looked like a harp, and another like a cello. Their music was accompanied by women's voices. I could hear their voice from the back, but I could not see them. I'd never heard such beautiful voices in my life. My whole body shook, but it stopped fast. At the same time, a tiny cloud filled with black dots floated in the hallway. I didn't pay too much attention to it because I felt my mind was poisoned. At that time, I believe that cloud followed me inside the house.

April 15, 2014. A full moon. I wrote a letter to Mark on the special paper I had bought in that spiritual store I had the two black candles and one of my own. After I finished the letter, I went outside. I lit the letter on fire and threw it in the air. It fell to the ground, so I lit it again. I went back inside. It was five o'clock in the morning.

Around lunchtime, I called my sister in Poland to tell her I had sent a letter to Mark. Suddenly, our conversation was disconnected. We did not know the reason; nothing was working. After a while, everything was okay. I told my sister that this was the sign that he had received my letter. There was something blocking me from remembering his whole face. I do not know his last name. All I know was that he was of Polish descent and from Montreal.

One night, I was sleeping when suddenly I felt as though something was covering my body and I had big wings. The left wing was choking me.

I woke up and immediately asked, "God bless all the souls. What would the soul like?"

He quickly answered, "You."

I knew it was Mark, and I told him to remove the wings as he was choking me, but he removed them only a little bit.

I asked him, "Who killed you?"

He was talking fast. He told me that he was working hard and was tired and had to go to sleep. I saw a black cape and big black wings but no head. At the same time, it was like I was watching everything from above. I saw him in a cave by the fire. It was dark and cold there. I have no explanation for that. He told me who killed him.

Chapter 3

After I sent the letter to Mark, I laid on the couch and covered my eyes, but everything was black and at that time I knew where he was. A couple of days later, I laid down on the couch and covered my eyes, everything was still black, but I saw a river. Instead of water, it was black lava. There were black bushes and a tall tent, dark grey and shiny. The covers closed very quickly so I could not see. It was awful. I prayed for him to get out of that place.

I went to a Polish church and asked for private confession. The priest was young. His name was Daniel, and he was very nice. He asked me what gift I had, and I told him a gift of love. I was crying as I spoke to him, but I don't know if he believed me. I told him he was young and would not understand that. I did receive forgiveness and when I got home, I prayed even more.

I was at a point where I kept everything to myself, even hiding from everybody at home. I started to choke. During Easter, I felt like I was choking and could not breathe. The doctor asked me about my past and I revealed part of my story. He looked at me and diagnosed me with anxiety.

I had a dream that Mark came to me. I asked him if he had received my letter, and he told me he had, but he did not show any happiness, at least it felt that way. It was like he did not have any interest.

He said slowly, "And you're going to be here soon too."

I was scared. I felt like I was losing my mind even more. I took a shower, got dressed, and went to the casino to distract my mind.

The following week, I went to a gala in dedication to Pope John Paul II. It was beautiful, but my heart was broken when I heard the song that the Pope liked. He had completed his mission, but I had not. I was embarrassed to be Polish.

For quite some time, the words he had said, "Do not fear," were stuck in my head. My dear Pope, it is thirty-seven years too late. I prayed to the Pope and Mother Theresa quite often. I ask myself, why? What was the reason? Was I afraid? Or was there an evil spirit inside me? I didn't know how to fight Satan.

I decided to go to the spiritual shop and buy more paper to write a second letter to him. I pretended not to see those witchcraft books, but it was impossible to avoid. I left that place quickly and decided to never return, as it was forbidden and against the will of God.

I heard a voice come into my head, saying, "Too bad, you would make a great sorcerer."

It sounded like voices of the higher witches. This happened multiple times. Sometimes I would ask myself, "Who gave me this curse? Who do I belong to?" I know I belong to God; I know I will succeed with prayer.

Could it be possible that once I wanted to be a witch, a healing witch? Who changed my life? Who did I become? I became a wife and mother.

Chapter 4

After being with Tony for years, I felt like he had ruined those years of my life, I was lost, confused and impulsive. I made rash decisions without thinking.

I started to write the second letter to Mark, thinking he told me who killed him, but never told me why. Deep down inside I knew the reason. He told me that I would be there soon. I thought, *Please do not take me away from my children and my grandchildren, they need me.*

I dreamt Mark was dressed casually, his eyes were squared, and he had a British accent. He walked slowly, and he played with a ball for a bit. In this dream, I saw his grandmother, and she said that we suited each other while she was having a drink. Nonchalantly, he went to the bar with my brother. I looked for them, but I couldn't find them. I went home in my housecoat, the one I'm wearing right now.

I tried dreaming of him for the past couple of nights, but I could not find him. My mind was in pain, and I would cry every day. Is it going to be like this for the rest of my life?

10:30 am: I was lying on the couch and could smell flowers. They smelled like bellflowers. That night I had a dream that he came to me. I saw a lot of people around him. He came to me and held me with his whole body. He kissed me gently, the way he was supposed to on the date that never happened.

He told me nicely, "We will make love later."

He was dressed in a light brown suit. I noticed that he had a scar on one side of his face.

5:20 am the following morning: I woke up because I felt hot. I felt that he was giving me his love. My body was moving; it was a different feeling and impossible to explain. When I got up, my body was sore, and my thighs were hurting; it was like I had made love to a live person. I couldn't believe it. I called my sister and told her the story; she could not believe it either. I called my friend and told her the story. She believed me. She had seen a program on TV about how ghosts can make love to humans.

I moved to a new house. On the weekend, I dreamt that he was at my house with my friend from Poland. He disappeared, and when he came back, he didn't talk much. He did not care. I prayed for him every day. In my head, I learned his last name.

I had a housewarming party and that evening. Upstairs, the hallway was filled with stacked boxed of unpacked items. We all heard a loud noise, as if a bomb had exploded. It was the unpacked items; they had fallen.

I said, "Leave my son's stuff alone. You are looking for me, but I am here."

Three weeks later, my dishwasher turned on by itself.

A bird started to sing, I went closer to it and asked, "Mark, is it you? Tell me something," a few times, but I only heard silence.

I was anxious to know what it meant, or maybe I already knew the answer. I didn't think he was going to hurt me again. Oh, Mark, if you only knew the truth, you would never hurt me. You would probably protect me instead of me protecting you.

God, you gave me my life because you know I am good and caring, that I can love, suffer, and carry everyone's pain. But why a curse? Was

I supposed to protect myself from Satan? I was afraid that I would be hurt by another man. It's possible that I was too weak and needed a big push. I wasn't afraid of his temper. You sent me an angel, who told me, "Maria, do it!" Why didn't you go inside my head and help me say the first words to Mark? Why didn't your angel go into Mark's head to say my name, Maria? The angel said to protect Mark, but he didn't tell me that Mark would hurt me.

God, I thought you left me. From above, You saw how brutal and painful the beatings were and I begged You for help and he stopped. You knew that I would survive. I never blame You for any of this, I love all Your angels and You, my dear God. Yes, I was upset that you sent me on a mission with Mark but didn't connect me with him. That was the choice of God and you, my dear Jesus. You knew that I would be strong enough to survive. Since my birth, you have given me a head of steel and an elastic body that heals quickly. Whatever beatings in life I took, only You and I know. You never allowed me to bleed because You, dear Jesus, spilled your blood for us all.

You gave me beauty and the figure of a model, but I have flat feet. Today my body is different, I am older, I am wiser, and my beauty is gone. At almost sixty-four years of age, I still walk quickly, like I have a motor inside me. Now I know You've never left me. If I went on this mission, it's possible that I could help bring the whole world to you. It was never on my mind to betray you. I needed more of a push and support from your side.

My sweet Jesus, I will always love You. It is possible that I loved Your mother more because she is a woman, and most of the time, I did pray to her. If You think I rejected you, then punish me and give me Your pain. I have Mark's pain every day, and I will take yours and everybody else's. After all, that's why you created me, but do not allow me to lose my mind, and never leave me when I die, I beg of You, my God. When you gave me this beautiful gift, I felt like I was blessed. Today I feel the same because I know You will never leave me.

While choking so many times from the pain and tears, I asked You, my God, to help me breathe, and You allowed me to catch my breath. I know You are with me and will never leave me. I feel you inside of me. If I knew you could take the time back, when I was supposed to be with Mark, then I would ask you to do so. Mark opened my eyes and brought me closer to you. Everything is now in your hands. I forgave everyone who hurt me in my life, and I would like forgiveness from those who I have hurt.

Dear Jesus, I want to be just like You. I am very happy being around people, but my soul is sad until I die. I beg of you, Jesus, do not leave me when I die. Remove everything bad from my children and my grandchildren and put it on me. I love my children and my grandchildren. My sweet God, sweet Jesus, did I predict my time, or did you?

My sweet Jesus, my dream is to visit the Holy Land and Vatican City. Will I ever visit there? When I die, will the bells ring for five minutes in Poland because that's where I was born? Or in Toronto because that's where it happened? Maybe in Montreal.

It is possible that I didn't know any other way, but I think it is worse to wait for that holy judgment. The holy court is in your hands. Holy Mother, will you help me? Jesus, it is so hard to carry everything. I don't know how you did it when they crucified you, nailing your hands and legs to the cross while you were alive. You forgave them and didn't curse them. What went on inside me that made me curse Mark? Or was it Satan? After he left, he was laughing. You, my sweet Jesus, knew how to deal with him. I was weak. It is so hard for me to fight with everything. It started with Mark's death; that is why I'm drinking, to ease my pain.

Every day, I questioned myself, "Who is Mark? Maybe just a young man looking for love? How did he die?" I cannot begin to imagine. I drove myself crazy with so many questions. I beg of You, sweet Jesus, do not allow me to end up like Mark. I would like to publish this book to be a lesson for others and for them to draw closer to you. Will I do it? I don't know. I don't know why I feel that when I die, there will be tragedies in the world. The clouds will rip open, creating heavy flooding. There will be tragic storms, tornados, typhoons, the grounds will crack from earthquakes, crime and deaths will worsen, the whole world will be at war. That's because the world has too much technology. People don't go to church; they don't pray, they don't celebrate. On Saturday, they party, and on Sunday, they work. They are turning away from you. People will be punished. Different religions are trying to take over, but in the end, I know You will succeed because You are the King of heaven and earth.

Chapter 5

As I was sitting in church for my nephew's wedding, I watched the priest performing the ceremony, and I thought about you, and how beautiful it would have been if that was you and me. But you were with me because I felt you touching my back. I felt that. I thought that you had forgotten about me, but you can come and touch me anytime; I am not afraid of you. I know that you are not going to hurt me. I feel lonely and unwanted for what I have done. My wish is to go back thirty-seven years and do everything the way it was supposed to be. Paying the price for what I've done is challenging. Nobody believes, just God and me. But God knows I am strong. I don't know how long I will be able to do this. Help me, please. Talk to me. Say something.

In the summer of 2014, I traveled to Poland for a wedding. I wanted to go to Krasnobrodu to see a priest that specialized in exorcisms. Is it possible that he may have answers? but he had a limited amount of time for me.

After I spoke to the priest, telling him what had happened to me from 1977 to January 2014, his first words were, "I don't believe you were chosen by God. You were chosen by Satan."

I went on to tell him that when I was five, I saw a man wearing a hat, he was watching me, and I stared at him before I ran away.

The priest then told me that He had chosen me because I'm good, humble, and kind. He said I am the child of God. He performed a special prayer on top of my head while I knelt, and then we said another prayer together.

The following day there was a mass for my brother. I went to church. My chest felt heavy, as though I had a stone resting on it. I thought about Mark and started to breathe heavily. I went to communion, and it helped me a lot. That evening, I began to think about Mark, and I started to pant like an animal. I prayed for him every day. I asked for his name to added to the Mass intentions along with my other deceased relatives. I think the priest removed the curse. It was hard for me.

Shortly after returning from Poland, I received news that my other brother had passed away, and I went back to Poland for the funeral. This was my third brother. I knew he had died for me. I said to my sister, "If I'm not going to die this year, somebody in our family will," and that's exactly what happened.

In Poland, I decided to return to the priest. I told him that everything was coming back, and it was hard. Again, I received a special blessing from the priest, and we prayed together. I told him that, when I pray, thoughts of Mark come to me in my prayers, and it confused me. It was like Satan had put a microchip inside my head that I could not remove. The priest told me to pray, and only dedicated prayer would help me. If only it were that easy. I told him that I had seen a psychic and she had told me that he was alive, and his eyes were different and watching me constantly.

Letter to the priest...

Dear Father,

From the bottom of my heart, I'd like to thank you for the help that you gave me. Thank you for removing the curse from me. I cut down on smoking and drinking alcohol, and I can control my habits better now. I never did drink alcohol during the day. I gained my appetite back because I was constantly losing weight.

Maria

I am alive! It's like God sent me a priest to help save my life. God, thank you very much for sending me Father Eugieniusza Derdzuek, I'm still fighting with Satan, and I know I will have fight him to for the rest of my life.

Chapter 6

Before I went to Poland in 1977, I predicted that the first man to kiss me would be my husband. It was supposed to be Mark. I had the fire of love inside of me, that would be dedicated to Mark. Now that I know the story of my life, I cannot blame God or Jesus. Not even Satan. Is it I who changed my life? Who was Mark? I don't know. I only know that he was becoming a lawyer and practiced law on my head. He had very blonde hair, that was practically white. He also wore a very blue suit; the same one he had on the night that he beat me. Was he Satan? I don't know. What does he have on the other side of his face? I don't know. I only know that I was told not to be afraid of his eyes, that they will change after we made love. I only know that I was in several accidents on scooters, motorcycles, and cars. I was even touched by lightning when I was thirteen. During one event, one of the engines on the airplane that I took to Toronto from Poland broke down. I ended up traveling for three days. I survived everything.

Being with Tony, my first love, it was something that I know now, was not supposed to happened, because I wanted to hurt myself. I saw Jesus in two different forms. One was of him carrying the cross; the second was the "Jesus, I trust in you" picture. I had a thought in my head telling me, "What you did, you were not supposed to do, and for that, you shall carry the cross for the rest of your life." Thank you, Jesus. I accept those crosses, and I carry them.

I read that Jesus once said, "I give a guilty conscience to those who reject and don't have feelings for my love."

The night that Mark attacked me I heard a beautiful voice that spoke to me. I never asked who it was. Was it a white angel? or a black angel? Everything was so fast that that I had blockages. I was so sure that Mark would not hurt me, but I was wrong. He hurt me tragically. He never said that he regretted anything, nor did he say, "Sorry, Maria." Not even in my dreams, yet I still think about him. I thought about him, prayed for him. Is he Satan, or does he have a master? I can find out, but it is against God. I don't know what I am going to do.

I'm asking God to behold me because I cannot behold myself. I feel like a part of Mark is going to be with me forever. A couple of times in church, I felt like he was invading me, but I told myself he would never take me from God.

"Never will you take me away from him, Mark. God's power is stronger than yours". At the same time, I feel it is hard to breathe before communion, but afterward, it feels effortless.

I was at the church for a special Mass, and the priest spoke of a story about Satan coming to God and asked him if he could have a person.

God said, "Yes, but the soul belongs to me."

I was confused, was he talking to me? Did I belong to Satan and my soul belong to God?

The priest brought out the holy sacrament and put it at the altar and said, "If anybody would like pray and ask Jesus and God for help, come to the altar."

It was beautiful. I went to the altar. I touched it and prayed, asking God for help. I started to cry, and the priest noticed.

He said, "I see good results already."

I cried. I hide that I cry every day, but you cannot hide that. I know people reject me quite often, sometimes my family, but I forgive everybody. It is sad. God, you are trying to bring me back completely to you. Will you do that? I don't know. Only you know.

Despite that, the priest from Poland told me not to make any more predictions. I cannot behold myself. My prediction for the next year is that there will be big winds and water, and I saw soil sliding, but I do not know where. There will be strong storms this year. The second time, I saw that the soil was cracking and opening in half. I wanted to see where, but I couldn't because both sides were obscured by fog, and I could only clearly see the center. There will be big tragedies in the world, and every year, it will get worse. I have always felt that I'm different from everybody else, and I have been told so, too. I feel lost and unwanted in this world. My life is worth nothing. Who am I? I don't know. I am not afraid of Satan. I am afraid of God. The power of Satan is strong. He's not afraid of churches, or priests. The priest I went to in Poland specializes in this. He prevented Mark from coming to see me, but Mark is still observing me in a different way.

The bird that sang that special melody, the same melody, I know that was him. Mark is a fallen angel with black wings, the one I brought to myself without knowing who he was. God forgive me; I did not know I was dealing with Satan. I will accept any pain for punishment. My God, you give me steel nerves. What I am going through sometimes feels like Sodom and Gomorrah, but my God, in time, steel wears down, too, and you will know when. God, the love I had for Mark, I never released to anyone.

Today, July 11th, 2015, I, Maria, pledge the love I had for Mark to you, God, your son, Jesus Christ, the Holy Spirit, and the Holy Mother. Protect me from Satan. I know I belong to God. I will serve God the way he wants me to for the rest of my life. I was in a church for the Mass, and I came home. I was sitting outside, and I felt something coming out of my body. It was halfway down my body, as if something were coming out of my stomach. I didn't move. When the feeling was gone, I touched my abdomen to see if it was there, and it was. I felt empty. It was a strange feeling and I felt lighter. It's a difficult feeling to describe when something is leaving your body. You don't know how to behave. I was scared. I went to lay down. Whenever I lay down, my mind would be coated with thoughts of Mark, but today, it was not. The heavy stone has finally been lifted. This was the day I was released from penance. I will never forget this day. Thank you, my God, my Jesus Christ, and my Holy Spirit.

I do not know how to behave or how to think. Two days ago, I put a cross on my necklace, but I could not wear it because it was in the way and felt heavy. Now I can wear it, and it feels good. The priest removed my curse, but I knew there was still something inside of me. He told me the truth: with true prayer, I will succeed. My dear God and Jesus, you patiently waited for me to pledge that love to you. You never had doubts about me, but there was a moment when I doubted calling upon Jesus for anything, and I cannot lie about that. My God, you forgave me, and you released me from living in hatred and anger. What was inside me was awful. Being cursed by Satan for thirty-seven years and the things he made me do were awful. Today I am a free woman from Satan! My dearest God, my dearest Jesus, my Holy Spirit, and dearest Mother Maria, I don't have words to describe how to thank you. Thank you, my guardian angel.

Today, July 13th, 2015, I went for a walk and started to feel the warmth of the air invading my body. I knew right away that it was God, Jesus Christ, or my Holy Spirit, and I said, "Oh, God, it's you." I felt so good, as though you were giving me back my love. You're giving me a second chance at love. You're renewing me. But it's a different love. Do you want me to love again? You also want me to love all the people just like you. I am laughing, and I have tears, but they are happy tears. You're talking to me.

I feel your spirit with me; I said, "God, I feel like I'm blessed."

You answered, "Maria, you are blessed."

I feel happy without nerves. I feel different, like a new Maria.

God, You're giving me a second chance in life. It's as if I have been born again. I am leaving this in Your hands. I have to heal my body. But will I ever heal? My dear God, You have a question for me, if I have any regrets. Today my answer to You is no. I do not regret anything. For You and Your son, Jesus Christ, I will do whatever You ask me, even if I have to give my life up for You. My God, that's the reason You created me. I know something else is waiting for me, but I don't know what it is, and maybe I don't want to know.

My Jesus, in 2015, I asked you to give us a mild winter, You granted my prayers. During the Holy Week, I asked you to not to allow me to drink alcohol, You granted me that prayer. When I went to Poland for my nephew's wedding, I asked you to make this day special with beautiful weather, and again, you granted me that prayer. On August 10, 2016, I prayed for rain. I knew how badly farmers needed it, You granted me that prayer too. I thank you for that and for the beautiful gift you gave me. So, my prayers have been answered.

You are introducing me to so many new saints, like Saint Jude. I started to pray to him every day. His words are: "People don't pray. When they need help, then they start to pray." He spoke true words, so I prayed, and he is helping me too.

I told him, "If you can help me, please, I would like to ask for a special request for my children and grandchildren. So far, I am very thankful for what you are doing for me."

I have also started to pray to my archangels, Michael, Gabriel, and Raphael. Maybe one day, I will need their help, and I know they will help me. I'm thanking them from the bottom of my heart.

My Jesus, I pray for the world on Youth Day, that everyone coming to Poland will be safe, and I pray that Poland will be safe. I ask you, my dear Jesus, to not allow anything to happen to anybody during those days. I thank you very much from the bottom of my heart because you gave me the answer that they will be safe.

My dearest God, my Holy Spirit. When I was down, You lifted me up. You gave me the strength to endure what I went through, what I am going through, and what I will face. I thank You from the bottom of my heart.

I will always pray to You and for You to succeed and be victorious. I will always love You, my God, my Jesus Christ, and all the saints. It doesn't matter what happens to me; I am not alone anymore.

What Is Love?

Love is beautiful
Love is blind
Love is painful and can make you cry
Love can destroy you
Love is evil
Love can make you suicidal
Love can kill you
But we still love

The Return of Satan

My dear God, the beautiful moments that I had didn't last too long, not even two weeks. Mark came back. The same thing started again. I began thinking, *What did I do? What did I wrongly miss? Did I not write everything? There are some things that I did not write.*

It was too painful to remember the pain Mark brought me. I placed a second curse on him: "Every time you make love to a woman, may you hear my screams, feel my pain and anguish. Your eyes and your temper will stay the same forever until true love rescues you." I felt such pain and anger. I didn't understand why, when he saw me, he did not talk to me.

When I finished my first story, I said, "Something else is waiting for me." I was right, but I never thought he would return again, and I did not know what to do anymore. I said to myself, "Maybe I'm not praying enough, or I don't know how to pray." Everything started to bug me. I did not know if I had enough tears. I am not good with technology, but I tried to do my best. I started to search about predictions and Satan, what he was capable of. I found the testimony of Roger Morneau—a trip into the supernatural. He was from Montreal. What happened to him in Montreal in 1946? I read the testimony and began to feel better. I said to myself, "I'm not the only one."

Roger Morneau's testimony opened my eyes more, but that was not enough. So, I searched for more. I found Father Pio. Who was Father Pio? I didn't know. I started to watch a movie about him, and I fell in love with that movie. His character touched me emotionally and I cried a lot. I know what he went through and that not too many people believed him in the beginning, only the ones close to him. He had stigmata. I said to myself, "That is the proof." I know that if he were still alive, he would understand me. I started to watch a movie about our Polish pope, John Paul II. I love our Polish pope, and I prayed for him every night. I decided to watch the movie about Father Pio a second time. He opened my eyes to so many things I didn't see before, as though he was helping me.

Soon after that, I started to pray for the seven gifts of the Holy Spirit. These prayers are beautiful, touching, and emotional. However, I must have complete peace and quiet. Sometimes I am awake at four o'clock in the morning, and I pray. I like peace. One time, I was praying the prayers from my computer, and the mouse and my glasses fell. My glasses broke, and as a result, something went wrong with the computer. But that didn't stop me. I knew it was Mark. I said to him, "You'll never stop me." I fixed my glasses, gluing them back together. The computer started working again. Mark said, "Maria, you are very clever."

I said to myself, "I have to get rid of him."

He said, "Maria, you'll never get rid of me." I told him my soul belonged to God, but he exclaimed, "But I still have you!"

I told him, "You beat me severely."

He said, "I regret that, but that's the only way I can communicate with you." He also asked, "What does God do for you."

My answer was, "He loves me."

When I was in Poland for my nephew's wedding. It was beautiful. I felt as though it was almost over. From out of nowhere, I heard Mark say, "It's not over until it's over." I was in disbelief.

I returned from Poland. I was sitting outside, and the bird was watching me. You see, Mark was still coming and trying to poison my mind and show me how beautiful my life could have been. To poison somebody's mind, that is Satan's specialty. But the Holy Spirit is blocking almost everything. Whatever Mark is doing, it is so hard, but now he's coming as a bird. He presented himself as a black bird before. This time, it was as a small black bird with an orange belly. Another bird followed him, but I know he tried to push that bird away. It's like the second bird that tried to stop him.

A couple of days after, two more birds appeared. I didn't know where they came from. They were bigger. I had never seen birds like that before. It was almost as though they were royal birds, with perfect shapes, clean, shiny, and big. They looked like birds from a painting. They watched me, and I knew they were talking about me. They seemed to be saying that they would leave me alone for now. I knew he was not alone; someone was helping him. At that time, no other birds came to my backyard. They would fly above, but they would not land in my yard.

When my mother was visiting me in Canada, she told me that when she was pregnant with me, she wanted to terminate the pregnancy, knowing that she already had many children to care for on her own. She was walking outside when a gypsy approached her. The gypsy said to my mom, "Come, let me tell you your fortune."

My mother said, "Go away, gypsy. I don't have money, and you don't tell the truth."

The gypsy woman said, "I know where you're going. You're going to get rid of what you are carrying inside of you but don't do it. Do not get rid of the pregnancy. It's going to be a girl, and you will name her Maria. You are going to be very happy and will spend the end of your life with her" but my mom never spent the end of her life with me. Who was that gypsy? Was she the one who chose me for Mark, or was she the white angel? I know God protected me all those years.

Or did my father sell our souls? Every time he got my mother pregnant, he would leave her for another women. He would impregnate them and start a life with them for a short period of time and then return. I never blamed my mother for anything. I was never angry with her that she wanted to terminate the pregnancy. My mom was still married to my father.

When I was eighteen years old, I saw my father in court to pay child support, but we didn't want anything from him. By then, he was already married to his third wife and had many other children, mostly boys. I wanted to get to know him, so I approached him, but I had the feeling that he didn't really want anything to do with me. I was hurt at that time, so I left it. Who was my father?

I started to pray more. "Blessed Spirit, grant me the gift of wisdom, that I always skillfully distinguish good from evil. Give me the gift of reason. I know the truth reveals as much as possible of human ineptitude. Give me the gift of skills. Everything I am comes from God, and He despises the vanity of this world. Give me the gift of counsel. I cautiously proceed among the danger of the present life and fulfill the will of God. Give me the gift of fortitude. I overcome the temptation of the enemy and endure prosecution. Give me the gift of piety. I may be enamored of meditation in prayer and in all that is related to the service of God. Give me the gift of fear of God. Even though I fear you, my God, I am afraid to offend you, only for your love. With all the other gifts, oh, Holy Spirit, give me the gift of repentance. I wept for your sins and the gift of mortification. I satisfied divine justice. Holy Spirit, fill my heart with good, love, grace, and perseverance. I live in a Catholic way and die with sanity."

So many things happened to me. But I forgot something very important. This voice from within, telling me, "The sooner I write this book, the better."

One night I had a dream that there were two groups of people, one on the left and one on the right. I heard them saying that if I were with Mark, I would be like Holy Mary. I was above them; I could see and hear everything. That didn't last too long.

Another night I had this woman come to me and say, "You have seven years to live, or maybe fifteen. I am not sure. Fifteen would be better." Then she disappeared.

Shortly after that I had a dream. I saw a lot of people with different faces, different eyes, and even red eyes. I saw Holy Mary, Jesus, and God. I was above them again. Nobody said anything. The gift that was given to me. I was told I would give Mark a son. I was told that I would get more healing powers. I found myself asking, "Is it possible that the child I give him would be the child to rule the world?"

I was in the kitchen, standing beside the sink. Suddenly I heard a loud bang in the sink. I nearly flipped. That was my answer. Nobody else was in the kitchen. Slowly everything started to be revealed. Who is Mark? Was he the prince of darkness? You see, I did talk to Mark, but I do not want to talk to him anymore. I would rather talk to God. But only I can hear the words, no one else. But the Holy Spirit is revealing the truth through my dreams. He wants me to find out on my own and to see the truth.

One night, I dreamt that I saw Mark. People were sitting in chairs, mostly women around my age. Mark stood in the front, like he was telling them something or teaching them. I was above them. He saw me and vanished instantly. The people did not know what was going on or where Mark had gone. They did not see me. Now he knows that I saw him and that I know the truth. But he is still playing with my mind. I have a lot of help from the Holy Spirit.

NOVEMBER 12TH, 2015

I was waiting for the bus, and I met this young man. We started to talk, and I don't know how, but we began talking about Satan. Then he said he was involved with Satan but that he didn't want to be. However, he was still half and half. He asked me what I had been punished for. I said, "For betraying him." My bus quickly came, and I had to go.

DECEMBER 13TH, 2015

As I was waiting for the bus again, a man was watching me. He was wearing a tribal hat and clean clothes, and he held a baseball cap, all one colour. He was going with this hat around the post, and he asked, "You like my hat?"

I replied, "It's nice."

He said, "I thought so. Come and have a drink with me."

I said, "No thank you."

He said, "I like you. You're kind of cute." He asked me what my favourite Beatles song was, and I told him I didn't have one. He asked me, "What is your favourite song?"

I told him, "Warrior."

He asked me, "Who sings that?"

I went, "Uh…" At that moment, I forgot.

He told me, "It's okay. Come here and drink with me anyway."

I again said, "No thank you." My bus came, and I got on. He reminded me of the man I had seen when I was five years old. I knew he was Satan. I felt that inside me.

Today I know the truth. I was not only cursed, but he had placed a spell on me. It is almost as if he put a curse on my family in Poland… My brother developed cancer in his throat in 2008 and died from a heart attack. My mum, she was healthy for the most part but in 2010, she broke her arm and she died from an overdose of a medication given to her in the hospital. My second brother developed lung cancer and had also had a heart condition, but with medication it was managed. In 2013 something went wrong, and he died from a pulmonary embolism. In 2014, my third brother died. He had a lot of problems with his health. I could not believe how my family had endured so many deaths. My third brother's death is the one that I predicted. Nobody believed me when I said that if I didn't die, somebody would die in my family. It breaks my heart. Mark knew I could not die, so he took my family.

Remember when I mentioned the tiny cloud filled with black dots? That cloud was filled with evil spirits that went into my house. The Mark's body was dead, but his soul is alive. I revealed all the truth to him. I dig him from the grave night after night to tell me who killed him. I pray for him every day, and every time I go to the cemetery, I light a candle for him. When the psychic told me he was alive, I had a compulsion to looked for him everywhere. I did not even believe the priest. Mark poisoned my mind so much. So many problems begin at home.

I dreamt that Mark was somewhere, surrounded by people. He kissed me and then told me he was going to come back to make love to me. As he waited to find another victim, his spirits played with my body. The more I drank, the happier he was. He gave orders to the spirits, and they did his job. He can make or do anything he wants. He can make you sick. You go to the doctor, and the doctor isn't sure what is wrong with you. He will send you for tests, and the tests will show nothing. Satan can send spirits and demons at night to chase you, and when you scream, nobody can hear you. He can make your body numb so you cannot move. He can do anything he wants; he can change his appearance. You can even get married to him without knowing. His power is beyond control.

Every night, when I went to bed, I would close my eyes and a movie would start to play in my head, that continued night after night........

I was there with him. I could see everything. We had dated, but not for long. We were in his place in Montreal. Inside, it was like an old castle, a spooky place. There were two evil statues that I was afraid of, and I told him that. The next day, they were removed. There were two extremely big dogs, and I told him I am scared of dogs. He said they would not touch me.

After dating for a while, we got married. He took me places, but it was a short thing. Then we would go dancing, but he would always disappear to take care of something. I thought it was wrong of him, that he always disappearing, but I could not say anything because that would create problems. One time, he took me dancing, and there was a skinny old man sitting in a wheelchair. Mark told me to kneel in front of the man and kiss his ring. I refused. He asked me again, and I refused once more. The old man said it was okay. We went back to his place, and Mark said that the man was paying for everything we have—including the jewelry I was wearing. I removed all the jewelry and said, "I don't want it." There was a fight; this happened quite often. The truth is, there was no escape. The tall gate outside and the dogs watching me constantly, that's how he brainwashed me. It was like he had placed some kind of chip in my head.

I am left with a scar for the rest of my life, a scar that never heals. There is no escape. He will follows me wherever I go. If you betray Satan, the penalty is death. I betrayed him, and he took it out on my family. He turned everything the opposite way against my marriage and my life.

My dearest God, my dearest Jesus, and my Holy Spirit, today I know I did not betray you. I only broke my promise to Jesus Christ. If somebody told me stories like that, I would not believe them in a million years, but it happened to me. My dearest God you placed with me a man who has two left hands because you knew I have two right hands. But this is not the only thing. You did it to protect me because he is Catholic, and it was the only way I could be safe. There are moments when I am afraid, but I remember the words of John Paul II, "Do not fear." He's helping me, too, and I always say to everybody he's like the right hand of Jesus. Today I will say that I am proud to be Polish. To Father Pio, your voice and your thoughts help me so much. I do not know how to thank you. You are like God to me. But I know this is not over yet. Please stay, both of you, with me until the end. I need all the help I can get.

January 2016

I dreamt, that the last time I saw Mark was in a place with a lot of people. Everybody was wearing pink. One girl had a bonnet with a longer back on her head. She was walking and carrying a wooden bowl. Mark was there, walking like he was confused of where he was. I was above them, and he did not see me. He was wearing a light blue suit; the same one I had seen him wearing in Montreal and in Toronto. This dream reminded me of a picture I found at a garage sale many years prior, everything was the exact same. I remember looking at that picture over 10 years ago and, I felt attached to it, but it was too expensive for me.

On Christmas, I received an angel holding a cross. It reminded me of myself, with long brown hair. It's like, it was telling me to get that kind of cross for my protection. My Holy Spirit, I cannot survive without you. So many times, Mark almost had me. But I said to my Holy Spirit, "Do not allow him to take me away from you and God." My Holy Spirit, you are beautiful, good, kind, and very patient. I am not very patient, and you know that. Please teach me how to be patient and relaxed. My holy spirit, so many things happened to me in my life. Now I know it is not over; You have released from the dark side, and the gift you gave me to see everything from above. I have to be prepared for worse. I accept all that you allow to happen to me. But I am begging you please, do not ever leave me.

2016

I, Maria, remove Mark from my heart and my mind. My heart and my mind, I pledge forever to my Holy Spirit. You are the one in charge of my mind. Guide, protect and control my mind.

In 2014, I felt so guilty for betraying God, for betraying Jesus. I started to pray a special prayer—the Mystery of Happiness. It is a prayer for one year, fifteen prayers a day, one for each of Jesus's wounds. He had 5,480 wounds. I prayed for all of them and more.

Today, when I lay down, I had a vision. I wish I had not seen it. I saw my body inside a coffin. I was dead. I saw for a moment, and then I vanished. I was above. I cannot explain why I vanished.

Sometimes I wonder who I am. It was emotionally disturbing. I cried a lot, but I remembered the words of my Polish pope, "Do not fear," and what I promised to my Holy Spirit. I accept what happened to me, and I must be strong. But sometimes I fail. It is so hard to do this. And I say to my Holy Spirit, "Don't ever allow Mark to take me away from you." I already broke my promise to Jesus Christ once, and I cannot allow myself to do it again.

You have to remember that Mark once served God. He knows the rules, but he broke them. He knows how to use his power, he can do and have anything that he wants, but he cannot have me.

To my guardian angel, when Mark beat me, I thought you were busy. But you stood up against me to protect me. You knew that God had made my head of steel, that I would have pain, but I would survive. Thank you, my guardian angel. I will protect my children, grandchildren, husband, family and those who surround me. I will protect them for the rest of my life. My prayers are stronger than ever.

And now that my Holy Spirit is revealing the truth and helping me, he's kind, patient, and so understanding. He teaches me every day, I say this prayer: "My Holy Spirit, beloved of my soul, I adore you. Enlighten, guide, strengthen, and console me. Tell me what I ought to do and command me to do it. I promise to submit to everything that you ask of me and to accept all that you allow to happen to me. Just show me what your will is. This is a beautiful prayer, just like you, my Holy Spirit."

I dreamed I was walking with a young girl. I guess she was my friend. It was cloudy, but I could see a road made of soil and very flat. On both sides were houses and verandas. I did not see the full houses. Four women were dressed in colourful dresses, like gypsies. They were talking and debating when they started to dance slowly. Suddenly I saw a thin layer of clouds and water above, maybe twenty or twenty-five centimeters wide. It was so thin that you could see through it. It moved quickly to one side.

Clouds formed a circle. There were so many of them and they were moving so quickly that they looked like they were boiling, almost like a tornado. I grabbed my head and said, "Oh, no! Oh, no! Oh, no!" and I lay down. The girl tried to help me, but I said I must be left alone. She removed my beret. Behind those women were three groups of men, one after the other. They all wore coffee-coloured suits. The first group was drinking and laughing. The second group was drinking and fighting. The third group was fighting with knives; it's like they were killing each other. But the clouds were boiling and came from behind them, swiping the men, all of them. There were no screams, no nothing. I have no idea what happened to those women; it was like they vanished. Who were they? Do I know any of them? Things like that are warning signs of bad things to come, tragedies and catastrophes. It was frightening.

For a long time, whenever I took a shower in the morning, I felt as though Mark was behind me, trying to touch me, but he could not. It was like it was forbidden to him. I said, "My heart belongs to him, and I will always have him in my mind."

In April 2016, when I pledged my heart and my mind to the Holy Spirit, the next day, I did not feel Mark anymore. Ninety-five percent was gone; the remaining five percent was the fear. Thank you, my Holy Spirit.

In the middle of June 2016, the birds were still coming for a short time, and then they stopped. On July 2, a different bird came, of the same family but older. He looked at me a couple of times and then flew away. Two days later, the same thing happened, but then it stopped. For how long? I do not know. What will happen to me? I don't know. I have to be prepared for the worst and accept it all. I know it's like I defeated him, but he's still tempting me. But it's a different temptation; he wants me to regret what happened. He is still watching me from afar as a bird or a human. That's what keeps me going. I will fight strongly to defeat the temptation and break the spell. I don't know if it's possible. Today I know this is the spell and curse he placed on me the day he beat me.

I had a dream. In it, I saw a field of beautiful grass. In the middle were flowers and a pond. On the other side were angels. They were tall and had big wings but there were so many of them. They were standing on what appeared to be a wooden stage, with four posts connected with light coloured robes. Their outfits were long and light brown. I wasn't allowed to go there, but I knew they were alive.

JULY 2016

I was sitting on the veranda when the bird came back. It watched me, but I ignored it. I had to be somewhere. I went for a walk, and as I approached the next street, the bird landed next to me and started walking alongside me. I couldn't take it anymore. I stopped and said to the bird, "Aren't you afraid?" The bird stopped walking and looked at me. Then it flew away.

I had another dream that my furniture was moving by itself. I said, "Oh, no, not this." Along with things falling, the dishwasher and dryer turning on a couple of times on their own, the even the doors opening by themselves.

You do not know how hard it is to write this book and to have gone through the things I went through—and will face again. Many times, you have to put a smile on your face and pretend that nothing happened. I am who I am. People have a right to express an opinion about me, but nobody has the right to judge me. Only God will judge me, nobody else, and perhaps he already has.

He chose me for this because he loves me. The more crosses he gives me, the more he loves me. So many times, I have cried. I cry for my children. I cry for my grandchildren. I cry for the whole world, for what they're going to face. There will be no mercy. Each year to come will get worse. You see, there is no technology to stop fires or floods, tornadoes and hurricanes, but most of all, there is no technology to stop the killings. There is so much hatred and crime in this world. Satan is taking over. Return to God, and you shall be saved. I told my friend how strong the power of Satan is. She said that she heard that the power of Satan is stronger than God's. My answer to her was, "NEVER!"

The power of God is stronger than anything else on this planet and in the whole universe. You see, God is winning. Nobody can defeat God, NOBODY! Not even Satan. People ask me why I wear black clothes and sometimes paint my nails black. I like it. Maybe because my favourite song is "Black Madonna." The Holy Mother with two scars on the right side of her face. That's the only way I can honour her because I love her.

I pray to the holy wound of Jesus Christ's shoulder. It is a beautiful and emotional prayer. People don't think about that, so it's unknown to most. Jesus wants me to tell Christians all over the world about it, so today I, Maria, am revealing it to all Christians. When Jesus carried the cross, he developed a severe wound on his shoulder, where three bones were visible, deep and the width of three fingers. That made him suffer and gave him more pain than any of his other wounds. Pray to his wound, and he will forgive you of your sins and grant you the grace that you are asking for, but you also need to say the Our Father and the Hail Mary three times. When I read this prayer for the first time, the next day, I could see those bones in his shoulder in my dreams.

There is so much hatred, anger, and crime today in this world. Let's pray to save the world.

NOVEMBER 2016

I went to the gym, and in the ladies' locker room, I saw a man coming from the back of the changing area. He stood and looked all over the locker room as if scanning the area with his eyes. It was as if he knew I was there. Believe me, at that moment, it was like I was frozen. I couldn't move or speak. Finally, he walked politely through the room. He said, "Sorry," and walked away. I reported him to the manager of the gym an hour later. She went through the surveillance tapes several times and told me she did not see any man go into or come out of the ladies' locker room.

Searching for prayers, I learned the words "Eli Eli lemasabachthani," (my God, my God why have you forsaken me) but I know my Jesus will never forsake me. You sent the Holy Spirit to protect me. Today I know the meaning of my life. Whatever I am doing, I am doing it for God.

MIRACLE OF SAINT CHARBEL

I found Saint Charbel in a book of many prayers called *Army of Precious Blood of Jesus Christ*. I wasn't sure if I wanted to pray to Saint Charbel. Perhaps it was his looks or his background, but something was pushing me to read about him.

When I read about him and what he is capable of, I was ashamed of myself for thinking of him in that way. I asked him for forgiveness more than once. I started to pray the Litany to Saint Charbel every day, and I asked him to protect me from Satan. I pleaded and begged him to tell me who is Mark (Satan) and who I am.

On January 13, 2018, around 8:00 am, I was walking in the kitchen, and suddenly I heard the name Malah. It was so loud, as if someone was standing behind me and shouting that name. I felt very strange. In the distance, I could see a flash of light in the shape of a church. But it was not an ordinary church—it was a church like the ones in the Middle East. For that short moment, it was as though I were in a different era. It was as strange as it was shocking. I was both dizzy and scared, and I felt as though I were a completely different person.

I remember the name, Malah, the angel of death. Oh, God, that would explain so many things in my life and why he was after me. So many times, I was close to death, but God protected me. I pray to Jesus; I remember the vision of angelic choirs, their beautiful voices. Jesus said, "He's sending angels and angelic choirs to protect people."

In the beginning of January, I found a gold piece on the floor in the shape of the letter L. For a moment, I thought maybe it was a toy that belonged to my grandson. I studied this piece every day. About a week later, I tried to kiss the cross I was wearing on my necklace. However, I noticed that I only had half of the cross.

"Oh, God," I said, "so this is the other half."

How could this have happened? The two halves of the cross had separated from each other. I took the cross to the jewelry store to be fixed. I cannot be without the cross. The cross is my protection. Maybe Satan can separate my cross from me, but he cannot separate my love for Jesus Christ because my love for Jesus is stronger than ever.

I continued to pray to Saint Charbel to release my mind from whatever spell Satan had placed in my head. It was like a microchip was placed inside my head. Every night, when I went to bed and tried to sleep, the same thing played over and over. It was weaker but like a poison in my mind. I prayed hard to Saint Charbel to release me from that. Saint Charbel's power is superior to Lucifer and his cohorts.

The next night, I went to bed and tried to sleep, and it was like magic. I woke up the next day free from whatever Satan had placed in me. The microchip had been removed. The next thing I prayed to Saint Charbel for was to help me with alcohol. I said to him, "I want to drink only once per week," but then I said, "Just please make me stop drinking." On the Saturday of the last week of February 2018, I said to myself, "I didn't have a drink today, and I didn't crave one." I could not believe what had happened to me. I always had a drink on Saturday.

Days, weeks, months passed, and I never touched alcohol again. My friends asked, "What happened?" I told them they would not understand. I owe my life to Saint Charbel for the miracles he gave me. I pray a lot and call him Golden Charbello. I also say, "Ora prono nobis," which means "Pray for us" in Latin. I must say, Satan has enormous power, and he is trying to poison my mind.

But I call on Saint Charbel and say, "Do not allow him to poison my mind," and every time I ask Saint Charbel for help, my mind is clear.

My dearest Charbello, I thank you from the bottom of my heart. I will always pray to you. You are my Golden Charbello

Jesus said that the Holy Spirit is forgotten. People avoid him. But we cannot be without the Holy Spirit, and that's why there is so much darkness in the world. Yes, my Jesus, the darkness I was living in and now I am free.

There is a prayer called Pray to the Lord Jesus. This prayer was found in the Savior's tomb. I looked for this prayer online and when I would say this prayer, more than once, a picture appeared in the middle of the screen, much bigger. Not only did a photo of Jesus appear, but also God our Father appeared twice during my prayers.

I talked to Jesus in March 2018, prayed to him, saying, "My Son." After that, I said, "Please forgive me." I said to myself, "What am I saying?"

Soon after that, I continued to pray every day, and I said again in Polish,

"My Son." Then I said to him, "You are old enough to be my son."

During the Holy Week, I said, "My Son," in English, the same week my feet were burning so badly.

I wanted to cry, but it was like something went into my head and said, "They made Jesus stand on fire."

I said to myself, "Is it possible that I can feel his pain?"

Soon after that, I felt relief. The next day, there was no more burning.

I believe that I can feel his pain, the burning of his feet. Because I said, "Allow me to feel your pain," Jesus is good to me. When I ask for help, he gives it to me. In many ways, believe me, it's like magic. I became so close to him. I confess to him my sins. And I asked for forgiveness. I did say I would try to bring the whole world to You. Can I do that? My prayers are strong, but that's not enough. I'm asking, no, I'm begging the whole world, all the nations, to pray to God, Jesus Christ, and the Holy Spirit to save the world and its people. Yes, the world may exist, but the people may not. You see, there are tragedies, catastrophes, and killings. If we don't pray, this will not stop. This is just a warning. The worst is yet to come.

Two years ago, I had a vision. I saw an atomic bomb exploding. Where? When? I do not know. Satan is poisoning people's minds. We must pray to stop him. And with prayers, we can succeed.

I pray for priests, I pray for nuns, I pray for people with depression and mental illnesses. The sick and poor as well as sinners. I pray for my neighbours. My prayers are strong, but not strong enough to save the world.

My dear Jesus, thank You and Your Father, the Holy Spirit, and all the choirs of angels. Thank you, Saint Charbel, Father Pio, John Paul II, Holy Mother Mary, and all the saints. Because of your help, I defeated Satan, and I am blessed in every way.

Today I will say that, when I die, I want the bells to ring—but only for your victory, Jesus. This is the beginning of the end for the world to come.

Part II

Death of my Husband

For quite some time, things became different at home. My husband even started going to the drug store to pick up his medication, and many times, he would buy milk, juice, chips, and other things. He never did that before. The only problem was that he could not carry the shopping from the car. Instead, he would call me to bring the stuff inside. After all, that was my job. Shortly after I got married, I felt like God placed something upon to me cook, clean, paint, and fix small things around the house. I never knew why, but today I know. God prepared me; he knew what I would face in life. Was my husband cursed or under a spell? Yes.

My husband started getting sick more and more often. He started losing weight. He began collapsing, and sometimes he would end up in the hospital. His driving started to get worse, and I told him he should stop. He was worried that he wouldn't be able to see his doctor, so I arranged for his doctor to visit him at home. The doctor arranged for physiotherapy. My husband spent a month in the hospital before coming home. His appetite began to improve, and shortly after, his physiotherapist started coming over, but he didn't always follow the rules.

He started getting weaker.

I told him, "You have to walk. If you don't, you will die." Then I repeated, "Walk, walk!"

One time, he was coming down the stairs, and he fell down them. I lifted him and told him to go back to his room, that I would bring him his breakfast and, if he got better, then he could try to come downstairs. But he said no, he wanted to go downstairs. I told him to try to slide down, one step at a time, and after the seventh step, he slid down the entire staircase. I thought he was going to die. I tried to call an ambulance, but he yelled, "No! Just pull me over." I called my neighbour for help, but after all this, he still ended up in the hospital. We had to bring his bed downstairs, and we placed it in the dining area, which was attached to the living room, so he could watch TV. At night, he would text me to help him. Yes, he did have a healthcare worker come, but they only came during the day.

Many times, I was tired. When a person is sick, they weigh twice as much. But that was my job—to help him. Usually, I would make him breakfast at 8 am, and he would eat and watch TV or play on his cellphone.

Winter was especially bad. One day, I went to shovel the driveway. As soon as I finished, I had to go and remove the snow from the sunroof before it collapsed. I had to borrow a stepladder from my neighbour and used a big broom stick and tried to remove the snow from the sunroof. There was so much snow everywhere. I had to make sure I placed the stepladder properly because, if I didn't, I would end up in the snowbank, and nobody would see me again. That day, the winter was brutal. I was removing the snow, and my right hand felt like it was freezing.

I said, "Oh, God, do not allow my hand to freeze. I must do this."

I begged Jesus; I also asked him to send me an angel to help me. Suddenly I felt a rush of warm air over my hand. I could not believe it. Everything on me was wet. I went back inside, and I had gotten a phone call from someone I had met once. She said her friend did roofing and he lived in my area. He could come over and take a look. But at that time, my husband was in the washroom, and the house smelled, so I was too embarrassed to ask him to come. I felt guilty asking Jesus for help and then rejecting it. I had to constantly remove the snow from both the driveway and the sunroof, maybe four or five times.

The next day, at five in the morning, I woke up, and my husband yelled, "Call the doctor!"

I replied, "It's five in the morning, and everything is closed. The nurse is coming at ten o'clock, so wait, or I can call an ambulance?"

He told me no, and I told him he had to be patient.

The nurse came, and she looked at his legs and said, "I don't like what I'm seeing. You have to go to the hospital."

He told her no and said that he wanted to see a doctor. She told him the doctor could come but did not have any equipment.

I said to him, "Go to the hospital. They will check you, and if everything is okay, you will come home."

He agreed, and the nurse left. I called an ambulance, and I came back to see him. He said he'd felt dizzy for a moment. The ambulance arrived and took him to the hospital. They said he'd had a mild stroke and there was a lot of water in his legs and lungs. They began to remove the water, and he developed an infection from the injection sites.

He grew weaker as time passed. I visited him almost every day. I was bringing him coffee and donuts. He kept insisting that he was fine. He did have a physiotherapist in the hospital. They said he would be ready to go home soon but his body was not functioning very well. He tried very hard, but the truth is, if you do not exercise, then your body is stuck. He had never walked much in his life, which explained why his muscles had gotten stuck and did not function properly.

One morning, I was praying. I said to Jesus, "I can't protect him anymore." I have no explanation for what I said, but a week or two later, I received a call from the hospital to come because my husband was asking for me. When I arrived, he had already passed away. That morning, we had texted at 9 am. He had told me the nurse had checked his vitals and everything was okay. I told him I would come later in the day, and he said it was better that way. I had been told in the hospital that he had suffered a heart attack and had passed away at 10 am. That was a shock for everyone in my family. The hospital was ready to release him. What went wrong? Only God knows.

When I came home, I prayed even harder, and I asked my Jesus to keep me strong. He did. I had to arrange everything for the funeral with my children. They were with me all the time during this period. I was surprised by how many relatives called from Canada, the USA, and Europe. He has a beautiful funeral and was honoured well.

I put so many things inside his casket: stamps, money—American and Canadian—whatever he had collected, including logos from the Knights of Columbus. The only thing I left out was his phone. My daughter said he didn't need it. Who was going to call him? We looked through it, I was shocked to see what had in it. He had contact with what seemed like the whole world. My granddaughter stayed with me the first week after his passing; she did not go anywhere.

My husband's bed was still in the dining room, and I debated what to do with it. One day, our dog jumped on the bed and started barking in the direction of the headboard, and then something seemed to push the dog off the bed. Believe me, I could see that the dog being pushed off the bed. I was home alone at the time, and I called my granddaughter to come home. When she arrived, I told her what had happened. I was scared. About a week later, I was outside, smoking, when I heard the dog start barking; and the same thing had happened, she was being pushed off the bed. I wasn't scared that time. I told my children that the bed had to be moved. I knew it was my husband pushing the dog away. He liked the dog, but he didn't like the dog being on his bed.

Maybe a week or two later, I was making pierogies. Suddenly I heard something in the chimney, as if someone were shaking hundreds of cans in a bag. The dog was barking loudly. I went up to the chimney and looked inside. There was nothing; it had stopped. I went back to my pierogies. Then it started again, and the dog started barking like crazy. I knew what had happened and why, but I wasn't sure if it was my husband or Mark, so I went and yelled, "Leave me alone!" and everything had stopped. I knew that my husband needed his phone. I should have asked then what the soul wanted, but I was confused.

The weekend came, and I was watching TV. Suddenly I heard a loud noise, like a buffet full of dishes had fallen. I ran upstairs. My granddaughter said it sounded like it was coming from downstairs, but I knew it had been upstairs. Nothing. I came downstairs, and I checked everything. Then I checked the washroom, but all I saw was that one of the pictures had fallen from the wall. The picture was very light, but the noise had been so loud. I hung the picture up again. I hung two pictures that day in the washroom. Soon after, the picture fell again, but it was a sound you'd expect to hear from the picture—not too loud. I removed both pictures from the washroom.

I knew one hundred percent that it was my husband. He wouldn't stop until he got his phone. I said to my husband, "I will get your phone and bring it to you." My daughter had his phone at that time, and she said she would erase some things from it. I told her not to do it, that I needed the phone as soon as possible. That night, I went to bed, and I lay down with the TV on and the lights off. But I could see what looked like a small silver ball moving quickly along the left side of my bed. I said, "Enough!" I got up and turned the light on, but there was nothing there. The next day, I went to my daughter's to get the phone, and I placed the phone in my husband's niche. My husband had been cremated. I apologized to him and asked for him to forgive me. Things stopped.

Maybe a month later, I was sitting outside and heard a loud noise of glass breaking. I went into the kitchen and saw pieces of glass on the floor. There had been no glass on the counter, so where had it come from? The pieces of glass were small and thick. It took me a long time to figure out where the glass had come from. A couple of years ago, I had removed the cover from the light above my oven and placed it on the back of the stove. I checked the back, and it was not slippery. I thought maybe this was my husband's way of saying thank you for the phone.

Sometimes I hear things upstairs. So, the dog and I just look upstairs and then look at each other but there is nothing. I forgot to mention—soon after my husband passed away, I felt like something was released from me. I felt lighter. I believe strongly that the spell was released from him.

Time went by, and 2019 was the worst year ever for me. In 2020, I was sitting outside, and I had a vision... I had heard a woman I used to know who had passed away say to another women as she rested her hands on her that she had left money in her will for me, and the other woman said in a gentle voice, "At least she will pray for you." Yes, I knew that woman. I had spoken to her when she was alive, and she did mention her will to me. I have been praying for her. Her lawyer never sent me a letter to notify me that she had left me money, but I will always pray for her.

On May 13, 2020, something pressed against my back. It felt like a thin piece of metal because it was cold. Shortly after, I felt the same feeling on my forehead. In that moment, I felt like I was frozen. How could I forget that day? I had a dream. In that dream, someone said to me that I should pray to Lucifer. There was a small shed that looked as though it was surrounded by boxes or something of that nature. I could not see anyone.

The big, evil birds started to come back. That would explain why my prayers were so heavy. Outside, I could see that birds had built a nest on the corner of my house. I heard the babies chirping. I noticed that it was a nest of those same evil birds. I was so upset. I went inside the house and grabbed my blessed salt.

I threw it on the tree where the big birds had been sitting and said, "Get off my property, Satan."

They flew away instantly, chirping and screaming. Later in the evening, I threw the salt on the nest. The next day, I didn't hear from any of those birds. I went and bought myself a holy cross for my own protection.

The year 2020 didn't start very well, either. Now we are dealing with the pandemic of COVID-19. I pray every day for this to end. I even went to church before they were shut down. I lay down in front of Jesus inside the church with my arms open, begging him to stop the spread of coronavirus and give the people a second chance—just like he did for me. I didn't get an answer because I already knew it's up to the people. The churches should have never been closed; they should have been open for people to pray. Everybody must pray to stop this. People are losing businesses and jobs. There will be more depression, stress, anxiety, and crime. Things will never be the same. I don't see this leading to anything good.

Things started to break in my house. I know I failed my Jesus, but I still have a mission to fulfill. Jesus is asking me to use the special book of prayers that I have to help save the world from eternal appearance. My sweet Jesus, I will try my best.

I want things to be normal again, but for now, I will continue to pray.

I pray a lot, but things are not going well, things breaking in my house, the chopping board falling off the counter. Maybe I pray too much, maybe I should cut down my prayers to half. I believe I said that to Jesus and the Holy Mother. A couple of days later I had a dream, I don't know what I was dreaming about, maybe angels playing in my head.

Then suddenly I heard a man's voice say "Hold it! Stop this dream for Holy Mary's announcement."

Then she appeared, beautifully in a white long dress, her words exactly were "Modlic sie nie ustannie bo bendzie biada." In translation, "Pray constantly because it will be woe".

She appeared in the same corner of my bedroom, where I have three pictures of her hanging.

On a different night I had a dream, I believe I heard the same voice saying, "Jesus doesn't look anything like the way they're showing him."

Knowing that I defeated him (Satan) he is still trying to come back, and I didn't understand why. After reading my special book, *The Army of the Special Blood of Jesus*, Jesus said He would be coming back, and now I understand why. Jesus also said prepare yourself to be rejected by people, friends and sometimes family. My sweet Jesus, how true word you have spoken.

In my story I've said that I saw angels and that they were beautiful. At that time, I didn't know why I was seeing angels or dreaming of them, but today I know why. According to my special book those are the angels waiting for people to call on them and to pray to them to help us overcome the evil of this world. Today, I, Maria, am begging the whole world and all the nations to call on that angel, to pray to that angel, ask the angel to help us and defeat evil. Together with the angels we are to call upon Michael the Archangel and the angel choir as they have enormous power. Angels bring light on earth. We can do this, Holy Mother said she can't do this on her own and neither can I, but together we can defeat worldly evil. I want this message to be announced all over the world. I want every priest in every church to spread this message to the people and bless the people with holy water after each mass, so the evil will not come to the church or the people. Prayer to Michael Arch Angel a must.

If we don't pray, there will be big tragedies and catastrophes its already happening, but we can stop this by praying.

FEBRUARY 11, 2022

I had a dream that I saw my body inside a casket, as I stared at myself laying there, I noticed my face was clear and younger. I saw Holy Mary standing at the head of the casket she was wearing a white dress and a royal cape that was of navy blue and purple. Her face was so beautiful, I guess she was there to guide me and to prepare the world, I believe this is the sign.

Over the years, I always wondered why so many things had to happened in my life, why I am so different. But now know the impact Satan had in my life. Mark is dead and he was killed by his daughter-in-law. I was never alone and always had Jesus' protection upon me. He never left me, like I thought he had. I also know that he's been testing me and believe me it was not easy what I have gone through and the challenges I will continue to face but again I need to repeat myself, He is my King, He is my Master, I love Him and will continue to serve Him.

My story may be all over the place, but I am not a writer, just an ordinary woman with a story to tell.

Maria